DAVID, YOUNG CHIEF OF THE QUILEUTES

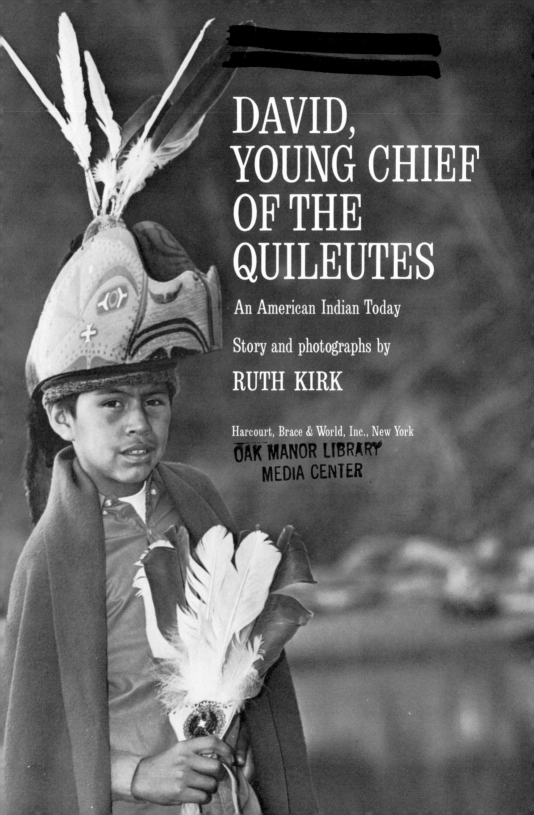

DAVID, YOUNG CHIEF OF THE QUILEUTES

An American Indian Today

Story and photographs by

RUTH KIRK

Harcourt, Brace & World, Inc., New York

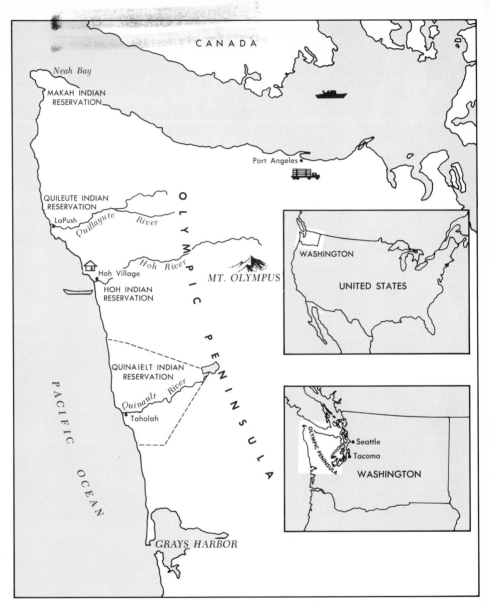

Library of Congress Catalog Card Number: AC 67-10206
Printed in the United States of America
First edition

Contents

VILLAGE LIFE   7

DAVID'S GRANDPARENTS   29

THE OLD DAYS   41

THE PARTY   52

Village Life

David Hudson soon will be eleven years old. Already he is an Indian Chief.

Great-Grandfather gave him the name *Hoh-ee-sha-ta* and made him Chief when David was only three years old. Great-Grandfather was Chief then, but he said: "Our people have come into a new kind of life and need young blood to lead them. I am too old." He picked David so that the boy could be trained all of his life for the job of Chief.

The Quileute Indians (Kwil-ee-oot) lived by hunting whales and seals from dugout canoes when Great-Grandfather was a boy, and by gathering berries and digging roots in the forest. They knew nothing of white men's ways because white men had not yet settled along the west coast of Washington, the home of David's people.

Now everything has changed. The members of the tribe still follow a few old customs, but more and more they live as other Americans do throughout the nation. They are United States citizens. They shop at supermarkets, cheer for their Little League team, and watch TV.

David has two names—his everyday name, David Rock Hudson, and his special Indian name, Hoheeshata. His special name is so old that nobody remembers who first used it or what it means, but the elders of the tribe agree that it always has been the name used by the Chief and passed along to his successor. David belongs to both the past and the present. He is the Chief of an ancient people in a modern world.

If you visited David, you probably would not find him looking like a chief. More likely he would be wearing rubber waders and standing knee-deep in the river helping his father to fish for salmon. Or he might be in the canoe, paddling to keep it pointed upstream while his father checks the nets. Or perhaps he would be washing the school bus with his grandfather.

David is too young a Chief to rule. A council elected by all the tribe governs the Quileutes, and they also are subject to state and national laws. When David is grown, he will lead by setting a good example for his people and by representing them at meetings, much as royalty in Europe lead without directly governing.

At present, being Chief means dressing up in a fringed shirt for special occasions and tucking eagle feathers into a beaded head-band with a blue Thunderbird design. It also means that David is honored at a big party each June 17, his birthday.

Once at school it meant something different—something funny. David was only in second grade at the time and didn't understand what being Chief really means. He was pushing his tray along the hot lunch counter one day, and he found spinach.

"No thanks," David said.

"Yes," the woman serving lunches said. "We all eat spinach."

"I don't," David answered. "I'm Chief, and chiefs don't eat what they don't like."

The teacher heard. "You're wrong," she told David. "More than anybody else, chiefs do what is hard. That is how they show the rest of us the best ways to think and live."

David ate the spinach.

Quileute Indians have been a fishing people for centuries. They fish today where their ancestors fished, working from the same kind of canoes hollowed out of logs. On lucky days David's father may pull two hundred fifty or three hundred pounds of salmon from his net, set at the mouth of the river where the fish leave the ocean and enter fresh water to spawn. Once David helped catch a great shining salmon that weighed sixty pounds, but more usual weights are from eight to fifteen pounds each.

Fish come to the river the year around. Spring salmon arrive in March—when "Elderberry Trees Turn White" (with flowers) according to the tribe's old calendar. Next come blueback salmon; then king salmon and silver salmon.

By the time that "First Rains Turn the River Muddy," in fall, the salmon are swimming past the village in a steady parade. Chum salmon join in as kings and silvers begin to dwindle, and with them come steelhead (sea-run rainbow trout that return to home water to spawn, just as salmon do). The steelhead keep coming all through the winter, until time for next year's spring salmon.

Smelt arrive at the Quileutes' doorstep, too—silvery finger-size fish that swim through the ocean surf to lay their eggs in the beach

sand. When villagers see them darting in the green crests of the waves, they wade out with dip nets to catch them. A canoe filled bow to stern with glistening, wet smelt looks wonderful, David thinks.

At ebbtide the Hudson family often dig clams among the rocks of the lower beach. A pitchfork and a strong back are all it takes. The clams are easy to find. In the days before white men came, the

Indians used clams as a standard unit of trade, somewhat as money is used today. A woman could trade four strings of smoked clams, with forty clams on each string, for a small basket or a necklace of seashells. Today the Hudsons build a fire of driftwood on the beach and bake their clams until the shells pop open, or they take them home and Grandma boils them to make chowder.

Time lies gently on the Quileutes' land. Fishing and clam-digging go back through the years to the tribe's early days. So does Hoh Village itself, David's home.

If you stood on the north bank of the Hoh River and looked across to the village, you would see approximately what white explorers saw when they first came to this coast two hundred years ago. Ten or twelve houses cluster against the low hill where the river rushes into the Pacific Ocean—about the same number as always, tribal elders say. The houses even look much the same (except for glass windows and brick chimneys) because Northwest Coast Indians traditionally built with wooden planks. Among these Indians a mark of importance and wealth was to have wider house planks than your neighbor did! Some were four feet wide and twenty feet long, enormous boards to split from logs using only bone wedges and a stone hammer as tools.

Douglas-fir and spruce trees still tower at the back of David's village, as in the old days, and elk roam in bands, grazing and browsing on forest plants. In front of the village, waves push scallops of white foam up empty beaches as they have for longer than men can know—longer even than Great-Grandfather can tell stories about.

David lives with his grandfather and grandmother Hudson and his cousin Cliff, eight years old. Great-Grandfather, the Old Chief who gave David his name, lives nearby in LaPush, the Quileutes' only other village.

David's father and stepmother live at Hoh Village part of each year, while the fishing is best, and with her tribe, the Warm Springs Indians, in Oregon the rest of the year. David stays with his grandparents instead of moving back and forth. Indians often have strong ties like this within their family: grandparents or aunts and uncles may be as important in a child's life as his parents.

After school each day David and Cliff like to play on the beach if they are not needed to help with the fishing. They run at the water's edge and explore the huge drift logs that wash from the

forest and onto the beach during storms. The logs pile in tangles like a giant's forgotten game of jackstraws. Sometimes the boys climb onto a stump and leap off into the air. They land with soft thuds in the dry sand, then climb up and jump again and again and again.

The beach never is lonely. When the tide goes out, the boys find purple and orange starfish clinging to rocks, quiet pools with green sea anemones and hermit crabs, and the tracks of deer and bear that have wandered from the forest to walk beside the waves. Sometimes there is a black cormorant to watch. Always there are sea gulls feeding in the soft, wet sand and calling to each other in a strange, wavering seaside sort of song.

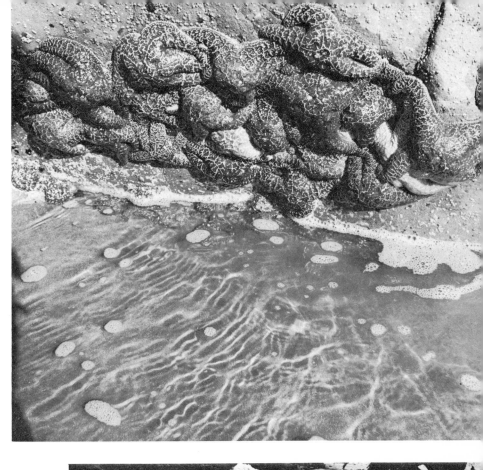

Often the boys see two eyes watching from where the surf swells and starts to roll toward land—a seal!

The Quileutes hunted seals in the old days. They ate the meat and oil and made bags and warm robes from the skins. When white men came, they joined in the sea hunt. As many as ten thousand seals were killed off the Quileute shore each year during the 1880's and 1890's—and the story was repeated all along the coast from California to Alaska and around the Pacific rim to China. Men needed tons of seal oil—and whale oil, too—because petroleum was not yet in common use and the main source of oil for fuel and lubrication was animals' bodies.

Nearly all the seals along America's coast were killed, and so were the sea otters and the whales. Then men saw what was happening, and the United States, Canada, Russia, and Japan agreed to limit their hunts and protect the future of the sea animals. Otters have never come back to the Washington coast; the last one there had been killed before the agreement was signed. But whales again migrate offshore by the hundreds, and seals dive and bob in the waves.

David's grandfather was a seal hunter. With two other men he would paddle out in a canoe far beyond land to harpoon seals as they slept, floating in the kelp beds. It was hard and dangerous work. The men would leave the village at midnight and not return until long after dark the next night. They paddled as much as twenty or thirty miles to sea, and then if luck and skill won, they might fill their canoe with ten or twelve seals. Or they might return with an empty canoe; or be swept ashore by storm and have to camp far from their village without food or blankets.

Today nobody in David's village hunts seals except when they swim into the river and eat salmon out of the nets. The Indians then get angry because it is hard work to set the nets and disappointing to lose fish that have been caught. Still, seals have such doglike faces and funny whiskers that David and Cliff can't help thinking it is fun to have one watch them play on the beach.

At 7:45 each weekday morning it is time to start for school. Grandpa is the school bus driver. He warms up the engine, and the village children race to climb aboard the bus. They drive thirty miles to the Forks School, stopping along the way to pick up children from ranches and logging camps. Everybody says that David's grandfather is the best driver in the district!

David is in the fifth grade. One day when the class opened their social studies books to a lesson about Indians, the teacher said: "Who shall we choose as student leader for this lesson?"

"Let's have David," the class answered.

They knew that David is from a different tribe than the one in the book, but they wanted him to lead anyway. "His ancestors were

here before ours came," they said, "and the Powhatan Indians in this lesson were already living along the Virginia coast when men arrived from England to found Jamestown."

In addition to social studies, David has classes in spelling, arithmetic, reading, biology, and Spanish. His biology teacher once let him help to measure a bear skull and an elk skull that someone found in the forest and brought to class. The bear's teeth were two inches long!

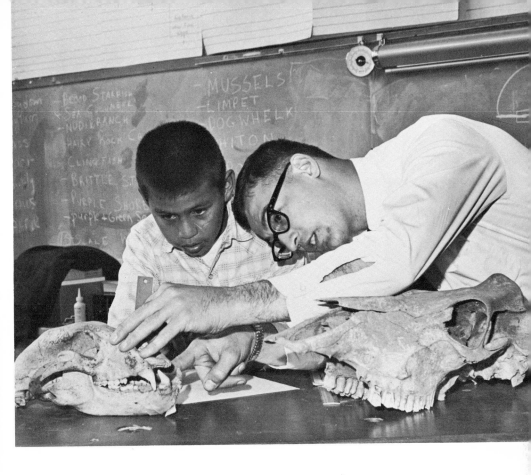

In Spanish class David learns to say *Buenos días* (Good morning) and *Muchas gracias* (Many thanks). But at home he is too busy fishing and playing and watching TV to learn even how to count to ten in the Quileute language. His grandparents speak it, as well as English, and they try to teach David. But Quileute is a hard language to learn, and young people see no use for it. Twenty-five or thirty tribal elders are the only people in all the world who speak it now. The language will die with them. David's grandparents are sad to think of it.

David's Grandparents

After David's grandfather puts the school bus away each afternoon, he works on the canoe that he is hollowing from a cedar log in the side yard. He is expert—one of only five or six Quileute men who still know how to make canoes.

He uses a gasoline-powered saw to cut the log into the rough shape of a canoe and to begin hollowing it. Then he changes to the same old-fashioned hand tools his father used. The boys hear the steady *whack, whack, whack* of Grandpa's ax and the lighter sound of his adze. They come to watch.

They jump inside the canoe and brush out the sweet-smelling chips that fly from Grandpa's strokes. They like watching and helping, but they are not really learning the art of canoemaking. Today's canoes will last forty or fifty years if they are cared for. Then there will be no more.

This is sad but also natural. Loss always accompanies change and progress. Grandpa begins a canoe with a power saw today, and this means that he has lost the use of elk-antler and stone tools. David's father adds a thirty-horsepower outboard motor to the canoe when he goes fishing; he has lost the full art of paddling,

although he still paddles and poles when the river is too low for motoring. By the time David has grandsons, the Quileutes probably will be using a different style of boat than the one he now watches being made. Canoes will be no more than a proud memory.

Grandpa's hands have carved many, many canoes, and his eyes have told him many, many times when everything is exactly right. He uses no pattern.

"As thick as a man's finger is just right for the top edge," he will tell you. "The rest of the sides should be two fingers thick, and the bottom three fingers thick so it won't split if you hit a rock in the river."

He shapes the hollowed log with a double-bitted ax and planes it to exactly the right thickness with his father's old adze. It has a handle of whale bone, with a wolf face carved into it as decoration. Its blade is from a Hudson's Bay Company ax—the old, old style of narrow hand-forged ax that white traders first brought to the Northwest over a century ago.

Grandmother Hudson is a famous basketmaker. She keeps boxes of cedar bark and bear grass and cattail beside a special chair where she can sit and look out the front window while she twines. She likes to work on baskets whenever she is not busy cooking or ironing or sewing.

Sometimes Grandma walks to a neighbor's house and sits with her in the warm kitchen, twining baskets and visiting. If you could step in the door, you would see the two women's fingers fly as they wrap strips of bark and grass in and out, back and forth. And you would hear their tongues fly, too! They like to speak the old Quileute words instead of English words. They know that the world has changed since the old days, but sometimes they can't help asking each other if the new life really is better.

"We were happy in the old days," they say. "We had food enough, and houses and clothes— and what we didn't have, we could trade for."

"Maybe trading was a better system than buying with money. We could always fish or hunt or dig roots to get something worth trading; but we can't always find a job and get money enough to buy what we need."

While the women talk, children who are too young for school play outside. Leanne, one of David's neighbors, watches over her baby cousin, Lisa. Her brothers play in a canoe, pretending to be fishermen like their fathers or seal and whale hunters like their grandfathers and great-grandfathers.

Indian women gather material for baskets in the forest. They know exactly where to find each kind and when to pick it.

"Go to Queets Prairie to pick bear grass in August," the women tell the girls.

"Cattail and swamp grass are ready in July."

"The best month for cedar bark usually is June."

They try to teach the girls the way their own mothers and grandmothers taught them, but they worry that the girls will not remember enough to pass basketmaking on to future generations.

They know that already the tribe has lost knowledge of how to dye grass with berry juice for red, alder bark for yellow, and sea urchins for blue. Today the women use dye powder from the dime store because it is quick and easy. But sometimes they wish they had watched and listened better themselves when they were young, so that they could make the soft old colors their grandmothers used to.

Each summer Grandma Hudson goes with her friends to gather bear grass. She invites David's stepmother, too, so that she can learn about Quileute basket materials. They are completely different from those she learned to use among her own people.

The women wear gloves to pull the bear grass because the stems are sharp enough to cut their fingers. Pulling grass is hot, dusty work, and the women's backs ache. Even so, they work all afternoon, until they have grass enough to last for a year and to trade to women in other tribes for other kinds of material.

When they finish picking, the women sit together in the shade to sort the grass. They put all the long stems together and all the short ones together. They also separate grass that is white at the base, where it pulled out of the earth, from grass that is red at the base. They will dye the two kinds differently.

Cliff likes to help his grandmother dry the grass when she gets home. He ties it into small bundles and helps her string them on a wire near the wood stove to dry quickly and evenly.

David does not pay attention to this any more. He did when he was little, like Cliff, but now he thinks that kind of work is for women.

One day when David's father went rabbit hunting, he happened to find a marsh with tall cattail just right for baskets. He asked two other men to go with him and help cut it for the women. Men do this because cattail is too heavy for women to handle—and, besides, Quileute women don't know how to take canoes up and down the river any more. They did in the old days, but now they know about Fords and Chevrolets instead of cedar canoes!

David's father puts the outboard motor on his canoe, and up the river the men go, with white water foaming out at the stern. They cut the cattail and load it in the canoe to take back to the village.

Cedar bark is men's work, too. They peel it from the trees in strips twenty or thirty feet long and drag these through the forest to the road like long, flat brown serpents. There the women pull the soft inner bark from the useless, stringy outer bark and roll it to take home and dry.

"Our mothers called cedar trees a gift from the gods," the women often will say. "The bark served for mats and clothes and diapers, as well as baskets. The wood made houses and canoes. Even the twigs were good. Men twisted them into ropes strong enough to tow a whale home from the hunt, far at sea.

"Everything we needed was at our doorstep: trees and grass and fish and seals and whales. Ours is a blessed land."

The Old Days

The Quileutes kept many of their old customs even after white people settled alongside them. Until 1900 they held a First Salmon Ceremony each year, carefully cutting the fish from tail to head with a mussel-shell knife. They always cut the fish this way; never crosswise and never with anything except a shell knife. For years they refused to sell salmon to white men because they feared the newcomers would cut them wrong and anger the Salmon People so much that they would come no more to the river.

After salmon for the ceremony were cut, the Indians cooked and ate them, giving thanks. When they finished, one of the men reverently placed the bones on the riverbank with the heads pointing upstream.

"Here you are, Mr. Salmon," everybody would say. "Here are your bones. Please be sure to come to our village again next year."

Nobody holds the full salmon ceremony now or worries how fish are cut—but sometimes the Hudsons like to do things the old way, as a family, so that David can understand how his ancestors lived.

One March when David and his father brought home the first spring salmon from their net, Grandpa suggested that they all camp on the beach and cook them the traditional way.

Grandma slit the fish with her biggest kitchen knife and opened them flat. Then Grandpa laid them on a framework of green alder sticks above a bed of glowing red coals. He cooked each side about fifteen minutes: flesh side first, then skin side. If you cook the skin side of salmon first, the flesh loosens and falls into the fire when you turn the fish over!

While the salmon cooked, Grandma made "sand bread." She stirred flour and water and a little baking powder into a dough like biscuit dough. She used no shortening or milk because sand bread is an old kind of bread from the days before the Indians had milk or any shortening other than oil from whales and seals.

Grandpa knocked the burning wood from a fire he had tended for six hours, long enough to heat the sand beneath it as hot as a bake oven. He buried the dough that Grandma brought him, covering it with three inches of sand.

"In ten minutes it will be baked," he said.

He was right. In ten minutes Grandpa lifted the bread with a long stick and brushed the sand from its hot brown crust. The sand fell away easily because Grandma had floured the dough heavily.

"If you flour the dough enough and have very hot, dry sand, the bread always comes out clean," Grandma said.

Cliff wondered. He spread butter and jam on a wedge of the bread and bit in slowly.

"Hey, it's good," he called to David. "No sand!"

David's great-grandfather remembers the first sand bread the tribe ever made, and he likes to tell about it.

"There was a shipwreck. Most of the tribe were up the river in fish camp, but I was still in the village here by the beach. I saw a big sailboat smash onto the rocks and white men jump overboard and swim toward our village.

"I was just a little boy about Cliff's age, but I knew what I must do. I couldn't paddle up the river alone in my little play canoe, but I must get to my father. He was Chief, and he must hear about the white men. So, I ran along the path through the forest.

"My father filled a canoe with dried fish and dried elk meat and paddled down the river to meet the white men. He said we must feed them and take care of them through the winter. At first, the white men were afraid when they saw us coming, but then they saw that we were bringing food and were happy.

"We helped them carry everything we could off their wrecked ship. There were big bags of flour and little boxes of baking powder. They both looked like strange white powder to us, and we could not guess why the white men liked it.

"Then they told us with sign language that the flour was to eat—and that it was best with a little baking powder in it! My father thought of this way to bake bread in the sand because of course we had no ovens. We always cooked in pits scooped out of fire-heated sand, or by dropping hot stones into wooden boxes of water."

Many ships have wrecked along the north Washington coast, and the Indians used to search for survivors and help them when they heard of a wreck. There was no warfare between whites and Indians, as in so much of the country. Indians simply moved over and made room when white settlers began to come. "The fish and the forests are enough for everybody," they said. And besides, they liked to trade furs and seal and whale oil for blue glass beads, warm blankets, flour, and sugar—and for nails and iron tools.

By 1855 so many white people had come to Washington that the governor decided to sign a treaty with the Indians. It set aside reservations and promised most tribes that they could always live where their fathers had lived. The rest of the land, the white men said, was now theirs.

This seemed strange to the Indians, and they did not like it. But they were too few to object, so they signed the treaty and did as the white men asked. David's great-great-grandfather signed for the Quileute tribe.

47

Not all treaties were like this. In other parts of the country, some treaties forced Indians to move hundreds of miles to strange new lands they did not know or like. Many Cherokee and Navajo Indians died when they had to leave their homelands. "The Trail of Tears," the Cherokees still call the experience, and the Navajos speak of "The Long Walk."

Great-Grandfather was a fisherman and whale hunter. When he grew too old for such heavy work, he leased his place on the river to a younger man, and he now goes himself only to finger the nets and help mend them—and to remember.

"Will you tell a story about the old days?" David sometimes asks when he finds his great-grandfather resting near the fish harbor.

"Shall it be about shipwrecks?" Great-Grandfather may answer —and then tell again about how the tribe learned to make sand bread or about other times that ships were wrecked.

"A call would go through the village," he will say. " 'Shipwreck! Shipwreck! Come help!'

48

"All of us men would leave our fishing or hunting—or our sleeping—and start walking the beach. We would go even if it was night and the wind was howling and the waves pounding. Sometimes we found sailors alive and gave them blankets and boiled coffee for them. Sometimes we found dead men and buried them. Once we found a woman and baby boy—the dead wife and son of the captain of a lumber schooner. That was in 1921."

Once Great-Grandfather told David about a chest of gold coins found on the beach after a shipwreck.

"That happened before I was born," he said. "Nobody in the village could think how to use little yellow discs, so boys skipped them across the water like clam shells. My father used to say that he could skip them ten or twelve times! There were no white people here then to tell us about money."

Often Great-Grandfather's stories are about hunting whales. Only Chief's families were allowed to do this.

He will bring out the worn cedar-bark bag he always kept his harpoon in and tell what it was like to paddle beyond sight of land and hunt for whales three times bigger than a canoe. Great-Grandfather first went whaling when he was only five years older than David. At eighteen he went again—and this time he himself stood in the bow and threw the harpoon. It struck just back of the whale's flipper, where the heart is.

That whale was the last one towed to the beach and cut up to provide the village with meat and blubber, for the Quileutes stopped hunting whales at sea and turned to white men's ways of living.

"It was about 1907 we got that last whale," Great-Grandfather told David.

50

Sometimes Eagle and Raven and Wolf and other spirits that always have watched over the Quileute tribe are what Great-Grandfather likes to tell about, and he lets David try on the family Thunderbird headdress.

"You are old enough to learn all this," Great-Grandfather will say. "Soon you will be eleven, and at your party we will show the painted blanket with our family's spirit story.

"You are Hoheeshata now; you are Chief. I am too old."

The Party

Bill Penn, a close friend of the Hudson family, beats a drum. *Thump, thump, thump.* It is time for the party to begin. Today is June 17. David is eleven years old.

Grandma and Grandpa Hudson stand at the door to greet the guests, and so does Great-Grandfather. Guests come from Hoh Village and LaPush, and from far away, too. Makah Indians come from the next reservation north of the Quileute Reservation, and Quinaielts from the next reservation to the south. Yakima Indians come from east of the mountains, beyond Seattle. Relatives of David's stepmother come all the way from the Warm Springs Reservation.

Most of the guests are adults. Two hundred fifty sit down at the long tables in the community hall to feast. David sits with them. There are flowers on each table and blue napkins that say "Happy Birthday." An American flag decorates the wall. It was given to the tribe by the U. S. government for their help in saving men from the 1921 shipwreck.

Children come to the party, too. Lisa watches from her baby board leaning against the wall, and Cliff goes to tickle her and

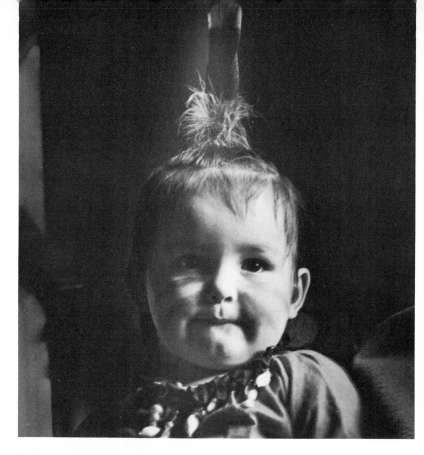

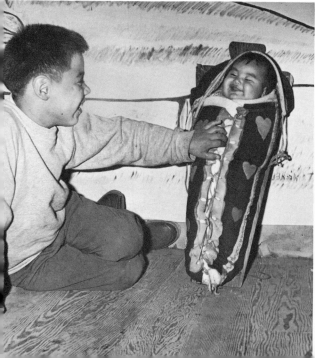

make her laugh. A two-year-old Makah girl called Princess Sea Gull sits wide-eyed. It is her first party.

Women cook salmon beside a fire outdoors. They split cedar sticks to hold the fish and push the sticks into the sand close to the coals. They cook the flesh side first, as the Hudsons did when they camped. When the fish is done, the women take it off the sticks and carry it in to the party in big pans. Children watch—and ask to lick the sticks!

Everybody eats all the salmon and boiled potatoes and cabbage and shrimp salad and bread that they want. Then it is time for dessert. Juicy red watermelons are cut and passed while Grandma Hudson puts eleven blue candles on David's cake.

"Happy 11th Birthday, Little Chief," the cake says in blue icing.

A baker in a city seventy-five miles from Hoh Village made the cake. He decorated it with a tepee and a warrior wearing a feather bonnet—the wrong kind of Indians! Plains Indians dressed like that and lived in houses of buffalo hides, but Northwest Indians carved wooden headdresses for ceremonial "hats" and lived in wooden houses.

Nobody minds the mistake, though. They think the cake looks beautiful. They sing, "Happy Birthday, dear David," in English and watch him blow out all eleven candles in one big *whoooosh*.

When the cake and watermelon are eaten, everybody pushes

56

dishes to the middle of the table and sits back to enjoy the rest of the party.

The master of ceremonies, Hal George, calls David to the front of the room.

"Here is Hoheeshata, the Little Chief," he says. He speaks first in English and then in Quileute and then in Makah. Mr. George is a good master of ceremonies because he can speak these three languages.

"The name Hoheeshata has been known on this coast since the old days," he continues. "The Old Chief did all he could do for us, and then he needed somebody to carry on for him, and he gave his name to this young boy. David Rock Hudson is our Chief now."

The guests start walking to the front of the room one at a time, bringing gifts. Some are for David. Some are for others in the family. A woman from the Quinaielt Reservation brings a red wool blanket wrapped in plastic.

"This is for the Old Chief," she says. "It is to keep him warm

in the back seat when the family drives down to visit us. We hope they come soon."

Many men and women give money to David. In all, he receives $135. Mr. George counts it and announces the amount. This is Indian custom.

"It will all go into David's bank account," Grandma says. "Thank you very much."

Other presents for David include books, a camera, a new wallet, a sweater, and a paint set. Cliff stands close and watches David open everything.

Then it is time for the Hudson family to give gifts to the guests. An Indian party always means gifts for everybody, hosts and guests alike.

David's party is the modern version of a *potlatch,* an Indian word for "giving." Families and whole tribes used to give enormous parties for hundreds of guests, some of whom had to paddle weeks to get to the party and more weeks to get home again. Potlatches often were so big that the hosts were poor afterwards. They gave away everything they had.

David's grandfather sits at a table with presents for the guests piled around him. Some are on the table, and some are in baskets and boxes on the floor. Mr. Penn helps with the presents in the old-fashioned way, as he learned long ago by watching his father and grandfather.

He calls out a name and the person stands. Then he tells everybody how fine this man or woman is.

"We are honored that you came to the party," he says. "The family of the Old Chief and the Young Chief thank you and ask you to accept this present." And he hands them a blanket or a basket or a five- or ten-dollar bill.

When all the special presents have been given away, Grandma Hudson walks up and down between the long tables and gives a towel and apron to each woman and a plate to each man.

Another kind of present is given at the party, too—songs!

Among Northwest Indians many songs are not simply to sing when you feel like it, or to listen to. They are very personal and tell about your spirit power. They belong to you alone. If you give a friend the right to sing one of these songs, you give him some of your power.

Two women and one man give songs to special guests. Then the Quileutes begin to sing songs that belong to the whole tribe. They sing in Quileute. Indians from the other tribes cannot understand the words, but they like to hear the songs. They know that these are the old rhythms and the old feelings.

Aunt Mattie, an old, old aunt of David's, sings and claps her hands with the men. The family is proud. Not many women know the old songs any more.

Cousin Dewey sings about a steelhead fish that he caught and asked his wife to cook the old ceremonial way. He had been sick, but when he ate the fish, he felt better.

After the Quileutes sing, it is the Makahs' turn. They are the largest visiting tribe.

Three men pick up deerskin drums and start the slow *thump, thump, thump* of the ancient drumbeats. Other men sing and clap.

Festus LaChester, one of the best Makah men dancers, puts on a Wolf headdress and a dance robe and whirls and stamps around the floor. He dances to honor the Young Chief of his neighboring tribe.

Makah children now come to the floor. They do a fast, running sandpiper dance. And a hopping medicine man dance. And a slow, spiritual, haunting Thunderbird dance. They wear costumes they have designed themselves and helped their mothers to sew. There are whales on almost every dress and shirt. This is because Whale was one of the most important spirits in the old days before white men came and changed everything.

Finally it is time to tell the story of the family's spirit blanket. It is painted with a young man just starting out in his life, as David is, and with spirits both good and dangerous that he meets on his journey through the years.

Great-Grandfather tells the story, because the spirits were his when he was Chief, and his father's and grandfather's before him.

The room is hushed except for the quavering voice of the white-haired Old Chief. Everybody wants to catch his words about Thunderbird and Whale and the other spirits. They are honored that he is telling them, but they will never tell the story outside this room or write it on paper. The spirits belong to the Hudson family, and they are the only ones with the right to tell about them.

Everybody listens and hopes that the new Chief Hoheeshata will find the good spirits to guide him. They hope the Young Chief will grow into a wise Chief and lead them well. It is hard to belong to two worlds—the old Indian world and the fast mechanical new world.

The Quileutes need their Chief.

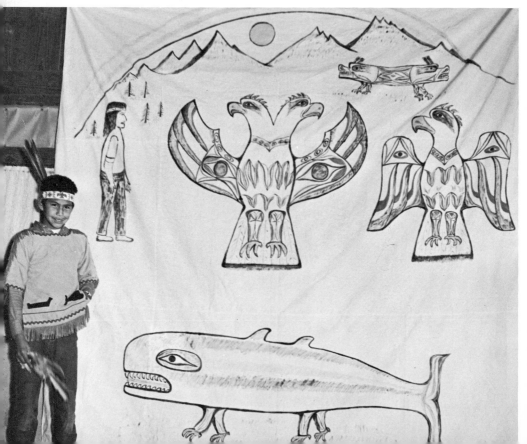